Val and Kip See Lin

By Carmel Reilly

Val and Kip got on the bus.

Kip sat on Val's lap.

Val and Kip got off the bus.

Kip ran to Lin.

Wag, wag!

Kip hit a lot of mud.

Lin got a jug at the tap.

Kip is wet.

CHECKING FOR MEANING

1. Who do Val and Kip see when they are on the bus? *(Literal)*

2. How did Lin and Val get wet? *(Literal)*

3. Do you think Kip likes visiting Lin? Why or why not? *(Inferential)*

EXTENDING VOCABULARY

wag	Look at the word *wag*. What is the last sound in *wag*? What other words can you think of that end in the same sound?
pats	Look at the word *pats*. What is the base of this word? How has adding *s* changed the meaning of the word? Find another word in the book where *s* has been added to make it mean more than one.
off	How many sounds are in the word *off*? Which letter or letters make each of the sounds?

MOVING BEYOND THE TEXT

1. Who do you like to go and visit? Why?

2. What are some different ways to travel to visit people?

3. Where do you think Vic the vet might have been going?

4. Kip the dog was on the bus. What are some places where you cannot take dogs?

SPEED SOUNDS

Kk	Ll	Vv	Qq	Ww
Dd	Jj	Oo	Gg	Uu
Cc	Bb	Rr	Ee	Ff	Hh	Nn
Mm	Ss	Aa	Pp	Ii	Tt

PRACTICE WORDS

Val

lap

vet

Vic

van

Lin

wag

lot

let

Kip

wet

Wag